HEALING MEMORIES

IN SECONDS!

Healing Memories in Seconds!

7 Ways That Work in Seconds!

Gary Sinclair

Healing Memories in Seconds

By Gary Sinclair

This book is from three decades of work in *Cyberphysiology* by Gary Sinclair as taught in *Life Clean Out* and *Restoration* trainings.

The word "heal" as used in this book is a word to mean, neutralize, balance, or remove the negative charge as in emotions or feelings as a part of the energy in a memory. It does not refer to a disease for which you should seek medical attention.

Published by Waterside Press
All rights reserved.

ISBN: 978-1-941768-73-0 ebook
ISBN: 978-1-941768-74-7 print edition

DEDICATION

To my wife Anne who has been through fifty-one years with me since meeting and knows the value of my calling to help people heal in mind, body, and spirit. From paralysis to healing in seconds, she has been through it all with me. No one said it would be easy.

Without God's voice in my head and the knowing of my calling, *Healing Memories in Seconds* would NOT exist. God woke me on May 27 at 4:30 AM. He told me to write this titled book as well as what would go in it that I already knew. Then on June 6th God gifted me with Soul Link.

To the thousands of people whose life has changed because of Cyberphysiology over the last three decades, your results are the living proof of how simple it can be to change. You represent my challenge to find even simpler, faster and more efficient ways to help people heal.

I honor those teachers who have passed on their gifts of knowledge so that I might re-interpret, condense, and make it easier for you to use. My NLP family is too numerous to name. It would be the last training I would ever give up due to the intrinsic value NLP has given me in understanding people.

A Word From The Author

Healing Memories in Seconds is the culmination of thirty-four years of research after overcoming fourteen years of up to eighty percent mobility loss from Multiple Sclerosis. In addition, this book is a result of being healed in fifteen minutes miraculously from one-third lung capacity that started as birth defects, to full and complete lung capacity. Now, at age seventy, the beginning of 2015, I am not on any prescribed medication. My personal general practitioner doctor for the last eighteen years would love to exchange bodies, and he knows all my history.

My understanding of life is so simple, that what I offer here is just that . . . simple. The things in this book you can do successfully too. Countless people from high schoolers to seniors have benefited from my understanding of "life as energy" in live events and *Restoration* trainings. You're here reading . . . it is now your turn. The student is ready and the teacher has appeared!

This book is calling to you, "Physician heal thyself!" in a new way. It will tell you that dis-ease is the beginning of disease. The very memory structure you know as life is who you are today. Thought is the occupation of life and with thought, you are about to be able to heal memories that bother you in as little as twenty seconds. There is no joke here, no gimmick, nothing to trick you; just you and the words calling to you to love yourself enough to put each process and technique to your ultimate test.

My thanks to the retired Neuroscientist, who admitted doing tens of millions of dollars in research in healing memories, as the Director at his Neuro Research Center. After being taught the best three chapters of this book, he had to agree his center found nothing that in any way even came close to what you will learn in this book. I can still hear him say, "This is so easy! And it works in seconds . . . it really does! Even my worst memory no longer bothers me!" After healing several more memories, he asked to remain anonymous while writing down the name of a friend he knew who immediately needed this help. Then we talked about new research he was doing in retirement in another area of science.

You will not find, as some will seek, pages of empirical research and documented studies. This book is not about others. It is about you. You are the one to do your own research and benefit from the results millions have found from such practices. As you follow the chapters, you will find a progression in education that will excite your Spirit with the possibilities of "setting the prisoner free!" In the back of your mind, you are thinking, "any memory?"

Well this gift of love is yours . . . it works! As I teach, I watch people heal thousands of memories every month. People just like you. Harmful things that once affected their lives so strongly come to a STOP!

You are not reading this by accident. Right now you need help with those memories you may never tell anyone about. Many with PTSD have already discovered the value these memories can serve, as those afflicted use sections of this book and feel the freedom that results. Even after years of seeking help, the answers lie within and are here now. Life is truly an inside job. May God grant you the wisdom and grace to know to continue with all possibilities. Inside of you are the seeds of miracles!

Perhaps you are one who helps others. This book and the additional training or even certification in *Restoration* will cause you to make a significant impact in other people's lives. There is no therapy like this! I know that after thirty-four years of research. My work in CyberPhysiology has been unique and a God-calling from day one when I was healed in 1980.

People who have seen a therapist and talked to doctors and counselors for years along with people who have received many forms of alternative therapies without the expected results could form a line with nearly no end. They would then tell you that it took minutes to heal those memories based on *Soul Link* alone.

Go . . . start now, so that you can get in line and tell your friends, "I found the answer and then it took 'twenty seconds' to heal my worst memory!" Just make sure you write and tell us what you did using this book at www.GarySinclair.com.

Bless you with Infinite Love and Gratitude!
Celebrate Life!
Gary Sinclair

Special Note: All processes are meant to work quickly and easily without getting complicated. If you find yourself laboring with any process, switch to another one so that you always do that which is easiest to heal the memory, emotion, or feeling for you. This book is about learning energetic healing possibilities that work in many ways.

TABLE OF CONTENTS

AND CAN IT BE

And can it be? The title of this book speaks volumes in terms of life changing potential for you. The truth is, I have been teaching these and many other energetic healing techniques for over three decades. Healing memories came early at the beginning of my learning curve and then worked into what has garnered two life-time achievement awards in Mind, Body, Spirit Healing. Today, I teach processes you can use to produce results in all those areas. Several techniques you will learn are so fast that you can even heal a memory in less than twenty seconds.

There was a time when people questioned, "Am I a spirit being having a human experience?" Today, with all the spiritual evolutionary changes in conscious awareness, people are seeking to know "why am I here" and "what is life all about?" Life as energy is now taken for granted. Scientists talk about life as an ever and ongoing creation in motion. What I have learned is there are much easier ways to take personal control of how your internal energy affects you.

In my searching for answers, one thing I realized is that we are all loaded with many types or forms of life sustaining and destroying energy. A major portion of this energy is memories that have positive or negative associations. For that reason, the decisions we make and the things we do, even automatically, have an inner positive or negative, charge or force, that allows or prevents our total success. Indeed, memories light the corners of our mind and energetically trigger responses that are empowering or disempowering.

Ponder that about eight-five percent of your thoughts today you also had the day before. Since like energy attracts like energy, far too many people find that today seems much like yesterday. And yet, we expect tomorrow to be different!

Since thought is the employment of life, ask yourself this question. What would it be like to get to a point in your life where you realize there is not one memory that still bothers you? That includes conscious and other than conscious memories. This book now contains some of the best of those tools and techniques so that you can begin to realize your life changing potential by healing memories in seconds. No question; that potential is here.

Knowing each technique about to be presented works, learn each one and use it for a day or two. Make sure you test each technique on many memories. You will discover there are some techniques you like more than others. Ultimately though, you will not need to use them all.

Each process is written as a chapter. It is presented in such a way as to give you the set-up first and then the process to heal a memory. A quick "how to" short list is referenced at the end of each chapter highlighting a procedure that is taught.

None of the processes are complicated. They may even seem too simple. My personal and most used one, *Soul Link*, will seem that way, until you use it. Your success is important, so once you decide which processes work best for you, think of all the memories you can heal, as well as the emotional help these processes can offer the seven billion people on the planet.

When I say heal, there is a specific outcome I have in mind. I believe that everything in life happens for a reason and a purpose, and it serves you. Therefore, what I have structured for your success will remove, neutralize, or balance the negative emotions and feelings in memories to where they no longer have a negative charge. You may continue to remember the memory. However, how it bothered you will have changed. For many it changes to where it is much like reading a page in a book about someone else's life. You have the blessing of knowing all about the memory, however the memory is so different in how it affects you.

Think of memories in terms of each individual memory having some form of containment holding it together on the inside. In order for it to be brought completely into conscious awareness, it must have some form of boundary holder to keep it complete. There must be something that keeps it intact inside so that it is not muddled with all the other memories when you bring it to consciousness. We could not function if we had all memories muddled into one. Gestalt therapy can also help explain how memories link and cause a reaction that relates more to the whole. In that work, you think of the memories much like a string of pearls. Energetically, many memories have found something in common to link them together.

To help in future explanations, think in terms of each memory having a box for containment. Note that when you bring a memory into consciousness, you notice the emotions and feelings that you have attached to it. In the framework of my research, I have discovered that emotions and feelings are very much a major part of the original holding component. Emotions and feelings are the positive or negative charge you feel about any memory. Although you may find memories that are neutral and positive, what we will work on and the reason for this book is healing those negatively charged.

When I seek to change a memory, there are several ways that are effective. The three format understandings I use the most are: 1) Blowing out the boundaries or containment of the memory energetically; 2) Changing the storage location perceptually with energy; 3) Going into all the perceptual properties or characteristic representations of how you stored the memory and changing some of those perceptions by how you see, hear, feel, taste, and smell the memory. I find these three methods work best for the energetic training related to *Healing Memories in Seconds*. At least, they are the easiest to put into print format. There are several other ways that I use to shift other forms of energy related to healing. I teach those as I teach people to do the healing work themselves in the two-day *Restoration* training you will learn more about in the back of this book.

So often, when people have completed the change to where a memory is neutral, they look at me and say, "Can it be that simple?" They then pause to reflect and answer themselves, "Of course it can . . . it worked!" When they can't find the PTSD memory, then they know it worked. For many, you may only remember a bit of a memory that reminds you something happened.

It is time for the miraculous to begin to take place. Healing memories in seconds is now available to you! As the chapter title suggested, **"And can it be?"** Let me teach you how! It is your turn to become the proof that it works. It is time to start your own research.

SHIFT HAPPENS

You will want to read this entire chapter before you begin the process. Then, as you reread or from your full and complete knowledge of what to do, complete the exercise process.

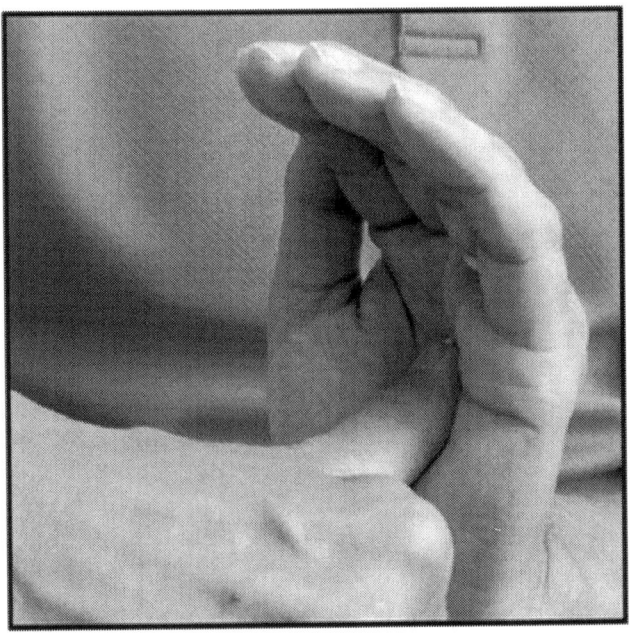

Take your thumb and rub it into the center palm of the opposite hand. Treat the process as though you are grinding something into the palm while using your thumb as the tool. Five pressing half-circle rubs will cause the energy of your body to pay attention to that area and allow what you ultimately are learning to be easier.

Now repeat that process by pressing the other center palm of the opposite hand.

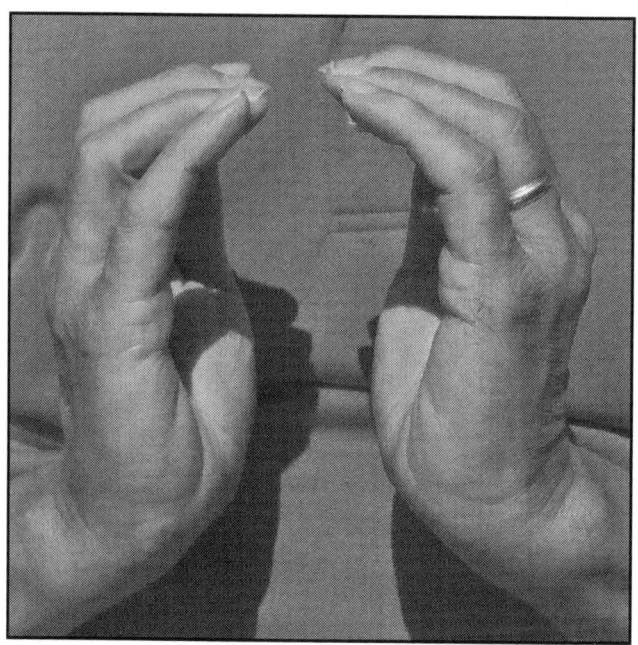

Allow your hands to form a ten-inch round ball like a child would hold. To do this, it is important that your fingers NOT touch and that you allow your hands and fingers to be absolutely relaxed so that it really is much like holding a round ball. Look at your hands and see that you have equal space between your finger tips and the space between your palms. This makes the center of each palm face the other.

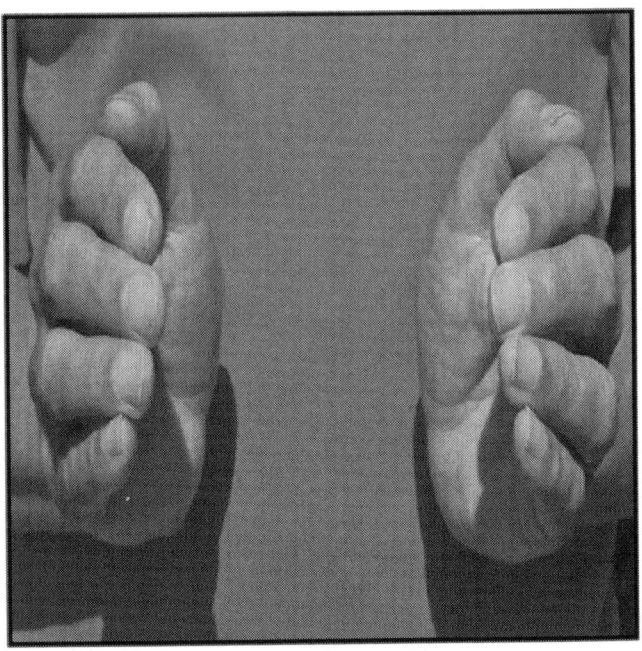

With your hands now steady in this position, allow yourself to feel the feeling of what it is like to focus your attention into the middle space of the ball. Then, begin to slowly move your hands toward each other as though compressing the ball while being sure to NOT let the fingers or base of the palms touch.

As much space as you moved your hands in originally, move them slowly back to where they were and then in the reverse direction until they have moved at least a few inches out from where you began. At this point, you might begin to feel a sensation of compression (in) and expansion (out).

Repeat this six to ten times or until you can really experience that feeling between your hands of compression (in) and expansion (out).

The energy you are feeling is "You" in there. Just as you have an aura that some can see and medical scan equipment can work with in diagnostics, notice that this is you energetically. In fact, have some fun and see how far away you can move your hands and still feel the compression and expansion. You might be very surprised.

When I am working with a group, I will often have someone be "one" of the hands, while I am the other. I will have them close their eyes after making sure they can feel me sending energy into their hand. I instruct them that when they can no longer feel that energy, to tell this to the others in the room. Although it can be done at greater distances, I generally stop at about ten to twelve feet and tell them to open their eyes. How little we understand how much and in how many ways we connect every day in energy. In part we do this just because we have that energy field around us and a heart emitting a signal with every beat adding to that field of presence as the energy of you.

Doing this exercise will aid in much of what you will do. You will feel the energetic changes in energy taking place before the work is even completed. As it moves, it will often expand or even contract.

Now let's figure out what memories to start the work of healing in seconds and exactly how you can learn to do it.

What Can I Heal

K nowing that everyone has memories, let's think in terms of a grading scale we can use while thinking about memories that bring up negative emotions and feelings. Everyone has had things in life that they would consider to be their best and their worst memories.

For what we will work on first, let us use a scale of one to ten with ten being the worst things you can remember happening. Recognize that most of your memories will be less than a grade of eight using this scale. Contract with yourself in this teaching and training to only work on memories in the three to four range for the first five times that you do each of the exercises. Once you have committed to learning and understanding the results you get from the first five, you will be able to focus more on what you are changing rather than trying to remember how to do it. When it is more of an automatic process, then consider testing memories going up to a five to six.

Do NOT test your skill on memories above a six until you feel that you have been successful in doing everything you can possibly think of in the

11

one to six range. If it has been there that long, it can wait for your proficiency to increase and thus make it so much easier on you to bring about healing in seconds.

At first when you go above a four, it may be possible that the change work did not complete, and that there are still negative feelings and emotions attached to the memory you just completed. You will note a shift did take place. Particularly, that what you were feeling before is not what you are feeling now.

As you think about the memory again, repeat the process to finalize the clearing. If it does not provide you with a feeling of neutral, do it as many times as needed realizing what you wish to no longer belong will shift more each.

Not working effectively and completely in one process at first is what happens to people who use any memory rather than following the three to four memory model instructions above. These individuals have not learned to master the technique and thus all the attention to what is necessary to shift the energy is broken up by trying to pay attention to how to do it. Whatever happens, make sure you take the emotions and feelings you have chosen to release all the way to that neutral feeling. And remember, repeating a process is not a sin . . . it is Heavenly in the end.

It is also possible that what you are healing as a memory has now brought about emotions and feelings from another memory for you to heal. You may be aware that one changed and now the new memory is related in some way. This new memory is what you pay attention to and heal next.

I remind you I wrote earlier that I have other ways to take care of many types of energy. I am not expecting most people to work on seven or higher memories using this teaching until they have had considerable practice and success in working with three to four range memories. Some memories may require professional help, and I do recommend that you seek it. For some people, memories in the eight to ten range have left deep emotional scars that have many layers to them. Thus, I only work with people experiencing that level face to face, in full live training like *Restoration* or privately.

A Ball

This one is simple, because you will know some of it already. Read the entire technique all the way to the end, then practice the process until you have mastered it.

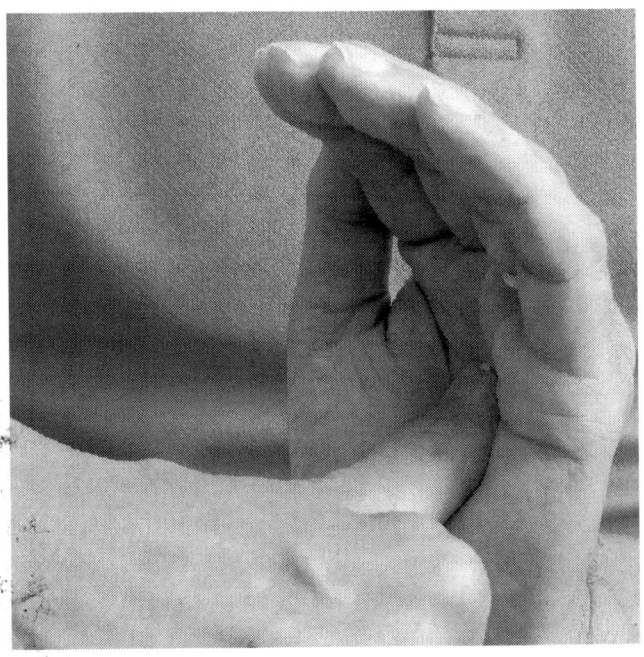

~ Set Up the Process ~

Take your thumb and press it into the opposite hand's palm and roll it around like you are pressing something into the hand. Repeat this process with the other hand with enough friction so that you are aware the centers of both hands feel it. This wakes up the energy flowing in your hands.

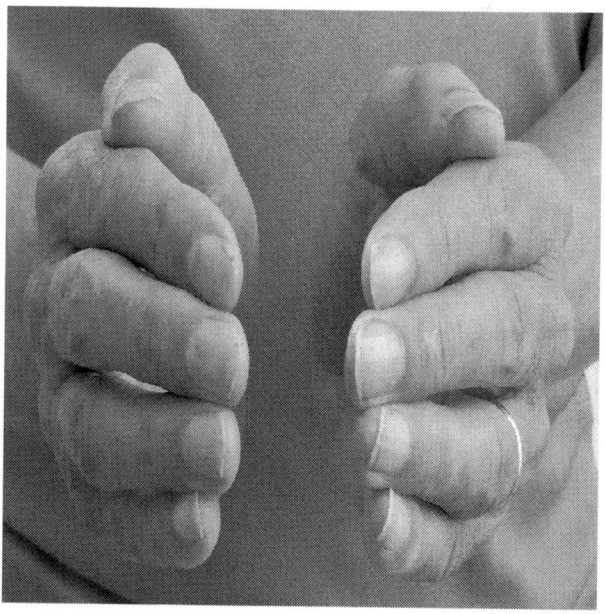

With your fingers now totally relaxed so that you have no finger joints taut and locked, form a round flexible ten inch ball between your hands about the size a child would use during play. Do not let your fingers or wrists touch. Allow your hands and fingers to form that round shape of the ball so that they are relaxed and look like they are actually pressed against the ball.

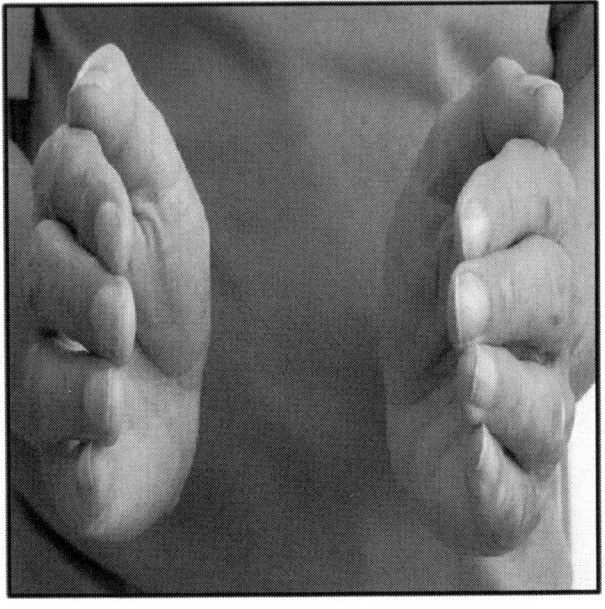

Now slowly and yet with intention to feel any movement in what is within your ball space, move your hands about two inches closer together without your opposite fingers touching. Then, repeat that process in the reverse direction so that you move your hands away from each other. Move them about three inches from where they started. Continue doing this slow, back and forth movement until you begin to feel the energy that is now flowing between your two hands.

You will feel this energy being compressed in one direction and pulled apart in the other. Keep moving them in and out as you play with this energy in expansion and contraction while recognizing you are feeling your energy between your hands. This is the life force that is in and surrounds you at all times.

Now, pick a memory in the three to four out of a one to ten range with ten being the worst. Be sure it gives you negative emotions and feelings in the range of a three to four. This is all about learning how to shift, dissolve, and remove that which you desire to no longer remain attached to this memory. This is NOT the time for anything above a three to four because you are in the learning stages of healing memories in seconds. It is important in your commitment that you agree that this training is specifically for a memory in the three to four range. Later you will be able to teach these processes to your children and others.

When you find the memory in the three to four range, discover what emotions and feelings come that you realize you wish were no longer there. Pay attention to those emotions and feelings with the intention to let them go by using this technique.

~ Doing the Healing ~

Holding your hands steady now, stare right inside the space of the imaginary ball you first created. Stare right into the middle as you intently remain aware of the emotions and feelings that have come to mind from this memory. Mentally hold onto those emotions and feelings as you recognize that they are connecting with the center of your ball. Remember, energy goes where you pay attention. Thus, as you pay attention to the center of the space, you are connecting that space with what you are thinking and feeling inside as well.

17

Holding that intention and with your focused attention in the middle of that "energy ball," begin to move your hands slowly inward to compress, and then pull them outward slightly beyond the size of your ball. Notice how, as you slightly feel those feelings of compression and expansion, your intention now is to remember those emotions and feelings that need to be unlocked, neutralized, and released.

Move your hands slowly to compress and expand three to four times. Then on the last compression, simply reverse it outward slowly to expand your hands out as far as you can continue to feel that feeling of expansion. Then simply let that feeling go.

Drop your hands and look around the area where you are. Tell yourself some of the things you notice in your visual field. Then take a nice deep breath and just relax.

Now think about the memory you were intending to change. Ask yourself "What is different?" Are you at a point where you can remember the memory with all the learning from the experience still there, with the entire negative emotions and feelings now gone? If the answer is yes . . . congratulations, you learn fast. If the answer is no . . . that is perfectly fine. Repeat the process again. This is all new to you. However, know that it has been proven to work, and it will work for you as you practice and improve your ability to move the energy. Your attention and intention will create this change. Congratulations! You just healed a memory in seconds.

Short Check List

1. *Negative memory*
2. *Create ball*
3. *Stare at center*
4. *Expand in and out*
5. *Expand all the way out*
6. *Look around to break connection*
7. *Check memory emotions and feelings*
8. *Memory should be neutral or do the emotions and feelings that have come up again*

EXPANDED
AWARENESS – THE BOX

R ead the entire technique all the way to the end, then practice the process until you have mastered how easily you can do it. It is important to remember your commitment to specifically use only a three to four range memory while learning a new technique. You are learning how to shift, dissolve, and remove that which you desire to no longer remain. You are learning tools you can use and teach to others, including your children. Now, much like the ball technique, learn to do the energy movement work first. Then the shifting process can be instantly rewarding.

~ Set Up the Process ~

Keep your face looking straight ahead, as though looking at something in your direct frontal vision.

Tilt only your eyes up to where you would consider you are looking at something out there more in alignment with where your eyebrows are. Check to make sure you did not move your head and only your eyes moved upwards.

Find any specific, small object that comes into your view that will allow you to completely focus your attention on it. For example, be sure there is not a lot of junk around the object that will make it harder to focus. In training I will use a recessed fan ceiling light casing, a ceiling fire sprinkler, a part of a chandelier, even one screw that holds an air duct plate in place, etc. Just keep it small in size and in a position so that as you face it, or move to face it, the object is in the eye position just mentioned.

Now allow you, as awareness inside, to stare at that object and stare ONLY at the object with the intention of allowing everything around it to defocus. When you are successful with knowing that all your attention is on one spot and the rest of the room is in a fuzzy blur, you may stop.

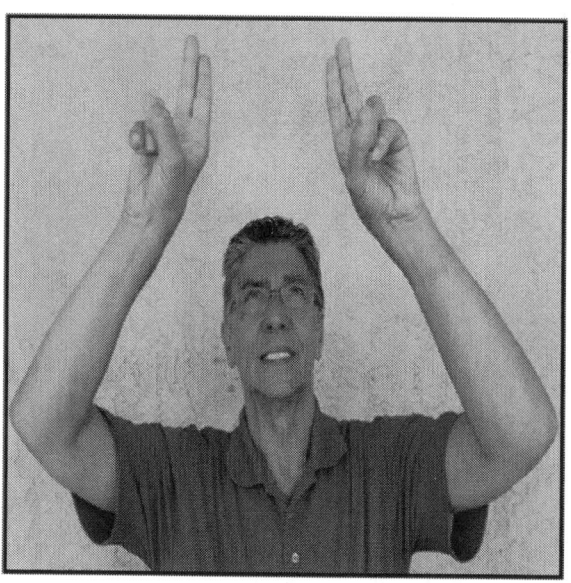

Now take and place your first two fingers on each hand to the left and right side of the object so that you can still clearly see the object while remaining in the face-forward position. Then allow the rest of the room to de-focus. Hold that position as you make the de-focus happen internationally.

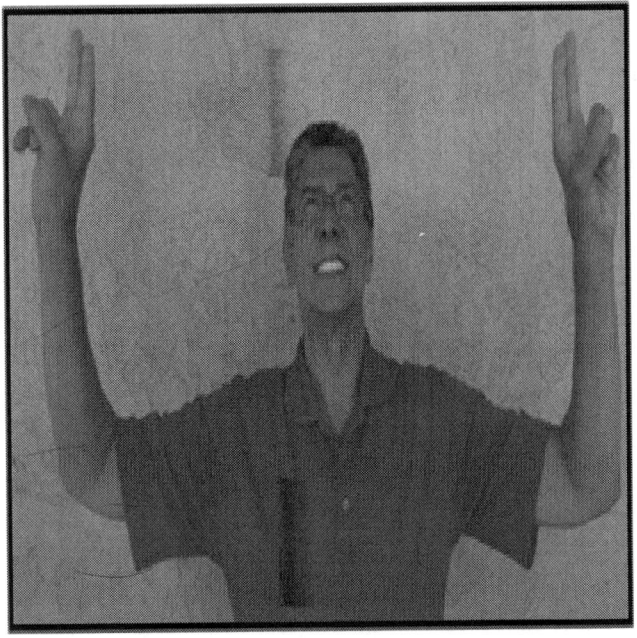

Next begin to move your fingers very slowly out to the left and right so that space around your object begins to open into the awareness of your vision while still remaining focused only on the object. Be sure to do this process slowly. A good speed to start the moving expansion of your hands is at about an inch per second.

As you allow yourself to experience this feeling of expanded awareness, note that you can see slightly above and below the object much like an expanding circle now opening up to include whatever comes into your vision of awareness.

Remember to stare only at the object, allowing you this feeling of expansion as your fingers move out and your awareness increases. Continue to move your fingers until they are close to the outside of your field of vision.

Stop. Look around the room to break away from the process, and then do it again. This time as you do it, and once you begin to feel that sense of expanded awareness, allow yourself to become consciously aware of the sounds you hear.

After you add in the sounds, add in the feeling of wherever your feet make contact and what your body is resting against. Note the pressure of those feelings of contact.

Before you finish moving your fingers all the way to the sides, add in the awareness of the sensation of the air coming into your nose or mouth.

Now that you have done this twice, you will find it gets easier from here. Do the whole process a couple more times. Make sure to add in what you see, hear, feel, and the movement of air into your body. In doing so, you make the healing process a multi-sensory experience.

As you are just learning this, do it two more times and shift your attention to noticing the feeling of expanded awareness as you move your fingers. Even after the first time, there is generally a very relaxing feeling that comes over your whole body. This is a process that you can use anytime to bring relaxation into your body.

~ Doing the Healing ~

Find a three to four level memory which you wish to heal in seconds. Be present in the now with the emotions and feelings about this memory that you desire to dissolve, release, or neutralize.

Since energy goes where you pay attention, as you focus on the object, you are connecting that space with what you are thinking and feeling inside as well.

Find your object again and place your fingers to the sides. Now as you stare at the object, realize that you know the above procedure and apply it to feel all that you experience about this memory you desire to heal. Feel those emotions and feelings and hold onto them as you allow the room to de-focus while staring at the object. Make sure your fingers are in the correct position to move.

When you have fully de-focused, while holding onto the emotions and feelings that you know you desire to remove, complete the process exactly as you learned with all the steps. Be sure to stare only at the object and allow your fingers to move slowly as you pay attention to your expanded awareness.

When you have completed the expansion hand movement all the way to the sides, stop and look around the room. Tell yourself internally the names of about five to seven things you see in your immediate space.

Now go back and check the memory. Notice what changed. If you have done it right, congratulations! You just healed a memory in seconds.

If for any reason you feel the slightest of any negative energy remaining, repeat the process until you know you are at a neutral energy level.

For most people this technique works perfectly the first time. After that, do it to more memories. However, pick up the speed ever so slightly with which you do the expansion. After a few days you can stop using your fingers and control the speed of expansion by concentrating as needed for complete success. Now you can heal memories without people even being aware of what you are doing. You can do it any time at any place.

By mastering this approach, you will be able to take a moment, like at a traffic light, and heal a memory or even those exhausted emotions and feelings of your day. Perhaps your day was "one of those." Now you can de-stress it before you even get home, so you don't take it out on those you love.

Short Check List

1. *Negative memory*
2. *Stare at spot and de-focus with fingers in position*
3. *Move fingers slowly out adding see, hear, and feel*
4. *Look around to break connection*
5. *Check memory and emotions and feelings*
6. *Memory should be neutral or do the emotions and feelings that have come up again*

USE THE ENERGY

When you buy a battery, it is charged with energy. As you use it though, you deplete it to where it will finally no longer work.

This is also true for any emotion and feeling that you have in your body. It has a holding component that can only carry so much energy. It has a life that can only last so long. Although it has a way of replenishing itself with usable energetic power, it still has a limit to how long it can function when brought into awareness each time.

~ Set Up the Process ~

With each memory you have already worked with, you may have discovered that there are common descriptive characteristic words that thread into your remembrance. If you use those descriptive words that come to mind right now, it would evoke the energy that has repetitively come to awareness associated with the word or words. This is because, like a memory, this energetic reaction you get from the word has a form of containment which is available energy you can use when something happens. The describing words become characteristics for labeling what you are feeling coming from this memory.

If you found whatever that emotion or feeling was in only one memory and not multiple memories, it would be different; however your life patterns will tend to pull whatever it is into your remembrance structure often. So the moment two or more memories have something in common with the other, they bond with the reactive pattern.

~ Doing the Healing ~

Think of whatever words that describe an energy that has been a common thread in so many of the memories you have healed already. What word or words would you use to describe what feeling those memories shared?

Now feel that feeling only. Allow yourself to just internally, and with intention, feel what arises. Not only feel it, but give whatever it is your fullest attention with the belief that you are not letting go. Continue to do just that . . . hold onto it.

There will come a point where you will feel like you lost it. That is the time to find it again, to reconnect, and give it your fullest attention all over again.

Continue to do this until you realize it just is not there. Then look around the room where you are and tell yourself some of the things you see. In doing so, you disconnect from the process you just completed. Then go back and check the emotion or feeling itself and see what comes energetically. Is that specific emotion or feeling no longer immediately there?

Congratulations to you! You just healed another part of memory structure. Now practice until you know this is one more technique you can easily do.

Short Check List
1. *Negative emotion and feeling*
2. *Pay full intention without letting go*
3. *Look around to break connection*
4. *Check emotions or feelings*
5. *Feeling neutral or hold onto again*

The Miracle

Awareness is the capacity to experience life within the framework of the complete soul of who you are. If you think of yourself as one total being of awareness, then you have to recognize there are "parts" of you in awareness that make you consciously aware of the smaller details of life, like reading this page. Each part of awareness is part of something larger than itself. The larger energy field is the very soul or total life controlling and supporting presence of who you are.

Some people would say "Awareness is what you are paying attention to while all of rest of life goes on." Whereas, I believe awareness is simply what you allow yourself to be aware of consciously. It matters not the size, shape, or structure. It is just that you are energetically aware of whatever it is as a part of the whole. To notice something, you create a smaller part of awareness. Were this not what was happening, you would quickly burn out your life sustaining energy. There would be no presence of you.

To help bring all awareness more into wholeness and then move into a connection of Oneness, we have to look at the process of what is actually taking place, rather than the content of what is coming to mind. Thus, we are taking what is happening and blowing out the boundaries of the containment so that what remains is awareness with this smaller part of awareness integrated back into the whole.

When you say "My Body" you are an awareness that recognizes you in presence there as a whole that has ownership of something called "My." If I asked, "Who said 'My Body'?" you might reply, "I said 'My Body'." Then the question becomes, "Who is 'My and I' on the inside that verbally represents itself in thought as being separate in identity from you?" "My and I" is that total part that we seek to help be more in wholeness with this process.

~ Set Up the Process ~

Allow yourself to become aware of a feeling or sensation much like you have felt many times before. Rather than picking a memory this time, go with just a feeling or sensation. When one comes, note a part of your awareness shifts your attention to this new feeling or sensation. This is a part of awareness at work within.

Notice all you can about this feeling. Take in as much detail as you can while remembering it is not the content that really matters. It is the process you are using to be aware of the content.

When you feel you fully understand this, we have something with which to work energetically for healing in seconds.

Go inside that awareness of this feeling and simply ask yourself to become conscious of where you specifically experience that feeling arise. Now remember it is being presented because a part of awareness is making you aware of this content. Where is that part of awareness that is making you aware? Notice that it need not be in the same location as where you got the feeling at all. The feeling is the content, and now we are checking in with the awareness that fed you that energetic connection. Where do you find this feeling of the "part" of awareness?

As you discover that part, because your energy field has been proven to exist in and around you, it is possible that the feeling may seem outside your body. There is nothing wrong with discovering that possibility. It can also be inches from the content feeling itself on the inside.

Notice too that there is a larger awareness of YOU that has also brought to mind that there is this smaller awareness. Yes, you can be aware of the larger awareness of you as well as the part from that larger awareness that is now working on your behalf.

Switch back to specifically paying attention to the part of you, as awareness, that gifted you with content.

~ Doing the Healing ~

Communicate now internally with this part of awareness by asking, "Is it possible within the framework of pure potentiality that you would like to begin to simply dissolve or expand back into the larger awareness of consciousness presence of who you are inside?"

When you feel the answer, allow the response to begin to take place immediately. Do not try to make anything happen. Just realize that the part knows home and is going there with no directions. This is a natural returning home that it wants to do.

However, if the answer is a "No," and that is not often, however is possible, then simply ask yourself, "Where is that feeling of awareness as a part that made you aware of that feeling of 'No'?"

When you have the location of that part, simply ask the same question you did before, "Is it possible within the framework of pure potentiality that you would like to begin to simply dissolve or expand back into the awareness of consciousness presence of who you are inside?"

When you feel the answer, again allow the response to begin to take place immediately.

If once more you receive a "No," you might consider that this emotion or feeling you are working on is involving much more in memory structure. You can continue to seek the part that gives you a "No," or you can experience the memory that comes from feeling the connected "content" and use one of the other processes like *Soul Link* on that memory.

If you continue to follow the "No," you will come to a part of awareness that will welcome the opportunity to dissolve and will do so rather quickly. Then as you check each one on down the chain, releases will continue as they each dissolve in the larger presence of awareness of you.

Now it is time to check to see if the part or parts have integrated back into the presence of wholeness of awareness. If it did, then peace and calm become present. When you are done, you can check for what was once there as "content" to now discover that it dissolved. Congratulations! Something else has healed in seconds.

Short Check List

1. *Locate emotion or feeling*
2. *Locate emotion or feeling awareness*
3. *Where is awareness*
4. *Dissolve or expand back into awareness*
5. *Check emotion or feeling*
6. *Neutral or check for another "No" level of awareness*
7. *Use another process if too many levels such as Soul Link or Move the Box*

Author Note: All processes are meant to work quickly and easily without getting complicated. If you find yourself laboring with any process, switch to another one so that you always do that which is easiest to heal the memory, emotion, or feeling for you. This book is about learning energetic healing possibilities that work in many ways.

CHARACTERISTIC
REPRESENTATIONS

In this chapter you will be given instructions on when to do the processing. It is not necessary to read the whole chapter and then return to do the process. Would it make it easier for the final outcome? The answer is yes. However, because of the subject matter, you may find yourself doing a lot of it while you read.

Submodalities are the characteristics we use to describe the internal language and representations we use to encode thoughts and experiences. In this chapter you will learn how to use your internal language for change. This will allow the emotions and feelings, like you have been working with already, to dissolve, release, or neutralize.

An example of your submodalities could be the language you use to describe a balloon. For instance, you might describe it as a light, yellow, flexible, coated containment of helium gas about the size of a beach ball with a piece of thin, clear, fishing line used to tie the opening base at the bottom so that the helium stays contained. These characteristics are described so strongly, that you now have a mental image of this balloon.

Thinking in terms of memories in general, you will discover that you have very specific ways of storing them and bringing them back to mind.

Your memories may come as a movie in life-like color or be images in black and white. You may find you see them near or far; to the left, right, center, down, middle, or up. Whatever comes into language is how you have formed that composite energy of containment. You are unique and one-of-a-kind. Thus whatever is right for you . . . is right for you.

The key in looking at those perceptions is that, for most people, changing even very little of your characteristic representations for negative memories, still releases, dissolves, and neutralizes the negative emotions and feelings attached. This chapter will be about discovering which potential language representational changes work best for you, so that you may narrow down your ability to start healing memories in seconds.

~ Set Up the Process ~

Spend whatever time it takes to find a memory that you consider to be one of the best memories of your life. Or, think of it as if you could relive a single memory completely in your life, this would be the one. It will help if other people are in the recall so that there are sounds and so that it is more daylight visual, rather than dark. Why are we using this memory? We use it because it will give you the best set of potential language representations for positive energy inside of you.

Give this positive memory your fullest attention so that you can see, hear, feel, possibly even taste, and smell how special it is. These representations will later be reused in another healing technique.

This is your book, and you likely already realize you have no intention of giving this one away. You will buy copies for your friends. You will want to mark up these next couple of pages. You can also use a separate piece of paper to write down your answers. Just make sure you keep your list. You will be thankful you did so you can refer back to it as you begin to pick up speed in the process. As you read the potential vocabulary in print, you may discover other words that come to mind that seem better to you than what is offered by me. Definitely write those in the margin or on your paper as well.

Some of what you will write there will seem to be so "not you." Everyone lives life to avoid pain or to gain pleasure. Some of these words that are so "not you," can be someone else's . . . as their pain is their pleasure. Just choose what is there or the best words that come to mind for your linguistic characteristics when describing your memory.

You will also find some of what I offer seems to make no difference to you at all. That is perfectly normal. I have worked with thousands of people and offer you a guideline below of what has worked for the majority of them. However, remember, you are a one-of-a-kind. When this list below is completed, you will be able to create your own custom list to make it easier for you to re-use and work faster.

Consider how you **SEE** the memory from these stand points:

> Movie or Sill Frame (Test for which feels best)
> Black and White or Color (Circle those with biggest feelings of being right)
> Image Viewed: Right, Left, or Center
> Image: Down, Middle or Up
> Brightness: 1, 2, 3, 4, 5, 6, 7, 8, 9, 10 (Dark1 to 10 Brightest)
> Picture/Movie Size: Large or Small
> Distance of Image: Up Close, Near, Far, or Very Far
> Speed of Motion: Still, Slow, Normal, Lifelike, or Fast
> You: In or Out of the Image
> Picture: In or Out of Focus
> Memory: Feel best as Framed Edges or Panoramic
> View: 3-D or Flat
> Colors: Particular Colors Stand Out (Name)
> Focus: Steady or Intermittent
> Angle: Angle You View it From (Name)

Consider how you **HEAR** the memory from these points:

> Direction sounds coming from: Left, Right, Behind, Front, or All Around
>
> Volume: Level of Sounds: 1, 2, 3, 4, 5, 6, 7, 8, 9, 10 (10=Loudest)
>
> Tone: Mellow, Soft, Sharp, or Hard
>
> Speed: Slow, Normal, Life-like, or Fast
>
> Word Sounds: Harmony or Disharmony
>
> Word Sounds: Regular or Irregular
>
> Inflections: Yes or No
>
> How long would you like these sounds to last to be perfect for you: Seconds, Minutes, Hours, or Forever?

Consider how you **FEEL** the memory from these points:

> Temperature: Cold, Cool, Normal, Warm, or Hot
>
> Texture: Soft, Silky, Smooth, Hard, Harsh, Rough, or Sharp
>
> Rigid or Flexible
>
> Relaxed or Tense
>
> Vibration: Bad, None, or Good
>
> Intensity: 1, 2, 3, 4, 5, 6, 7, 8, 9, 10 (10=Intense)
>
> Where You Feel Most: Gut, Stomach, Heart, Throat, or Head
>
> Steady or Intermittent
>
> Internal or External

Size: Small, Medium, Large, Extra Large
Shape: Ragged, Smooth, Square, Round, Rough, Rugged
Weight: Tons, Heavy, Pounds, Light, or Light-as-a-Feather

Consider how you **SMELL** the memory from these points:

Smell: Perfume, Flower, Forest, Ocean air, Bouquet, Holiday
Go ahead and be specific in naming something with this smell. Example: Fresh Christmas Tree
Smell: Favorite Flower (Name)
Smell: Favorite Food (Name)

Consider how you **TASTE** the memory from these points:

Taste: Spoiled, Rancid, Sour, Bitter, Spicy, Flavorful, Sweet, Honey, Chocolate, Holiday Food
Taste: Favorite Meal (Name)
Taste: Favorite Dessert (Name)
Go ahead and be specific in naming something with this taste.
Example: Spicy like my grandmother's Thanksgiving turkey dressing.

Now you should have a complete list that gives you linguistic submodalities that represent positive energy in you. You could do many positive memories and discover that the bulk of this list repeats itself. Although it could possibly be used to help others, it is for the one-of-a-kind you.

The last part of this setup is to find that memory in the three to four range that you wish to heal. For the purposes of learning, remember your commitment to learn the process using three to four level memories first. This way you get to focus on the learning so that you can do it easily.

With this memory getting your full attention, you might begin to show yourself how differently you store memories with negative emotions and feelings. You also might gain more insights by looking at the list and noticing differences in the first three categories of SEE, HEAR and FEEL. There may be many differences. There can also be just a few.

~ Doing the Healing ~

The listed answers you wrote in the book or on your hand-written sheet are what you are now going to use.

As you continue to give your present attention to your three to four range memory, you will start at the top of your list and follow down the page.

The first line says "Movie or Still Frame." Regardless of what you perceive as you view this three to four memory, make sure that it is now what you circled or wrote on your sheet from the previous exercise.

The exception is that if you change it, and it gives you a negative feeling, switch it back. For example, Relaxed to Tense or Movie to Still Frame. If the response you get does not increase the positive or neutral feelings, then switch it back.

As you continue to stay focused with your memory, move down line by line and keep making all of the switches in representation.

As you do work with this memory and others, you will improve your skill. Place a mark near the ones that you realize make the biggest changes.

When you have completed the page, stop thinking about the memory and disconnect from it by looking around the room and telling yourself some of the things you see, hear, or feel.

Even as a first-time learning experience, when you think about the memory again, you will discover that as you do, what no longer belonged is now released, dissolved, and neutralized. Congratulations once more! You have healed another memory. Although this process took longer to use, the end results of what you can now do using it only increases your capacity to begin to use higher than three to four level memories and achieve miraculous results.

I had mentioned marking those things that made the biggest difference. If you did, take another memory now in the three to four range and simply make only the changes that you circled as being most effective. If necessary and you did not do it before, do the full memory again and make sure to mark those that make a significant difference this time.

When you are done, you may discover that only using the marked items will be all that is required. With practice you may be able to shorten your list further or even group the items for more efficiency. Some people make a quick paragraph they can read. Just make sure the paragraph covers all the areas. Or, applying some of what I know other people have used, they may tell themselves for example: "Make the memory in color, normal life speed, in focus, while seeing you in the movie." Although there are many representations in there, this statement works to save considerable time and may cover all that is necessary.

These approaches may not be right for you, so remember to get creative as you find your best responses. What you need to pay attention to are the results. Does the faster version do just what the slower version did? If the answer is "yes," congratulations on having the process down to healing memories in seconds.

Short Check List

1. *Negative memory*
2. *Run your page list*
3. *Check memory*
4. *Memory neutral or do pages again*

Soul Link

R ead the entire technique all the way to the end and then practice until you have mastered how easily you can do the process without thinking about the mechanical movement.

This technique has proven to be one of the most successful ever presented for use in healing memories. Although you may find it simple, the end results leave most in awe regardless of the strength of the memory!

~ Set Up the Process ~

You will use both hands in this procedure. As you look at your right hand, palm facing you, all the basic surface area you see is going to be used to come in contact with the back side of the left hand. This is the area from the finger tips to the wrist connection. The right hand is the moving point of contact, while the reverse area on the back of the left hand is where you will make intended, sensory contact by touch.

Earlier, when you made the round ball of energy, you could feel your energy as you allowed your hands to remain close to limp. Your fingers and hands were relaxed to form the ball. In this way, the energy could easily flow between your hands and into the space you were creating in the middle. *Soul Link* uses this flow of energy again in a different way.

Relaxed hands in a loose, rounded looking position are necessary until the entire procedure is completed. If you straighten out your fingers, you stop some of the changing flow of energy necessary to complete the healing memory process.

Place your relaxed right hand, tips of your fingers, up against your curved and relaxed left hand. To do this, your little finger will be aimed straight at the row of knuckles on the top middle of your left hand. This location is the beginning point of contact for each repeated round in the process.

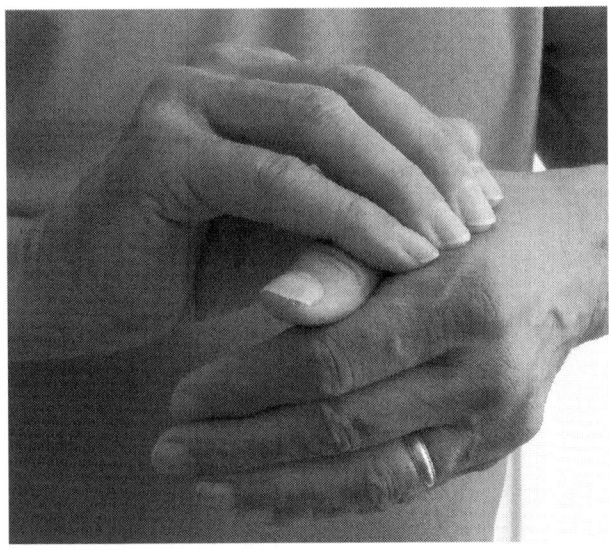

Once you have both hands relaxed, with your thumbs up against your fingers which are held together, begin to slide the fingers of the right hand up and over the wrist area of the left hand, following the line of the knuckles, with an intention to rub and feel all the area of the wrist. As you do this, note your little finger intentionally glides over the complete first row of knuckles. Your right thumb will glide close to where the wrist connects to the arm. Both hands are to make as much skin to skin surface contact as possible.

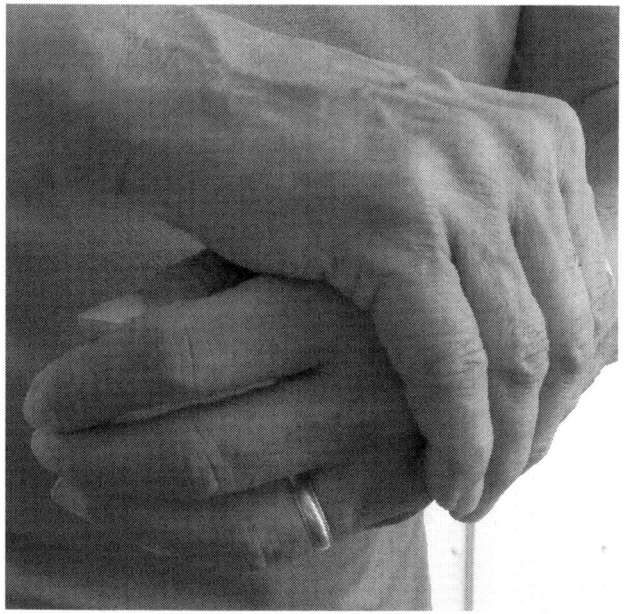

Allow the skin on the back of your left hand to feel all the contact of the palm of your right hand as you slide your rubbing hand. Stop when you are just past the full hand and palm area. You will have glided your entire hand all the way past the top side of your left wrist. It helps to think in terms of the knuckles on the back of the left hand as being the target line for the little finger to glide over.

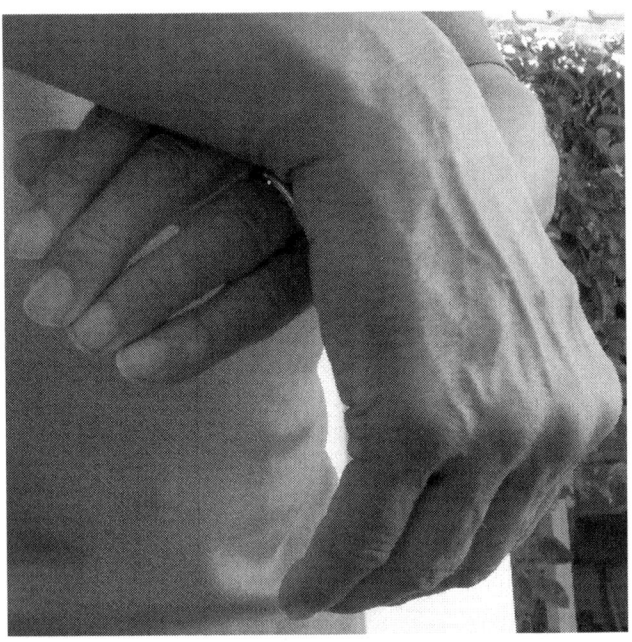

When you have completely slid across, you will feel like you could drop your right hand down at the wrist joint over the left hand's outside edge. Dropping the wrist is not necessary; this is only to explain how far you will go in sliding as you intentionally feel the rub across with both hands making contact.

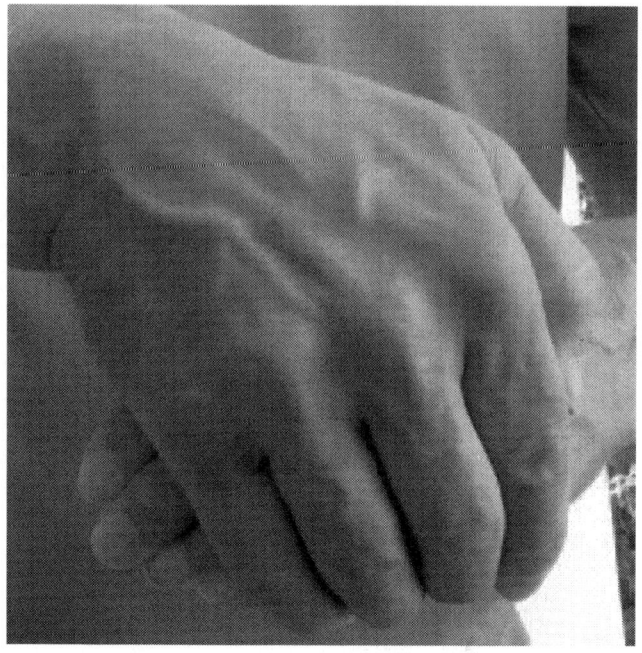

Check by coming back to the starting position again. This time, as you slide your relaxed right hand across, you can notice how much you will feel the connection. Set your intention to make rubbing contact as you feel all the connective sensations that are possible. Be sure you used the alignment of your little finger on your right hand going over the top line of knuckles as a way of allowing the placement of the hands to make the best use of the energy contacts.

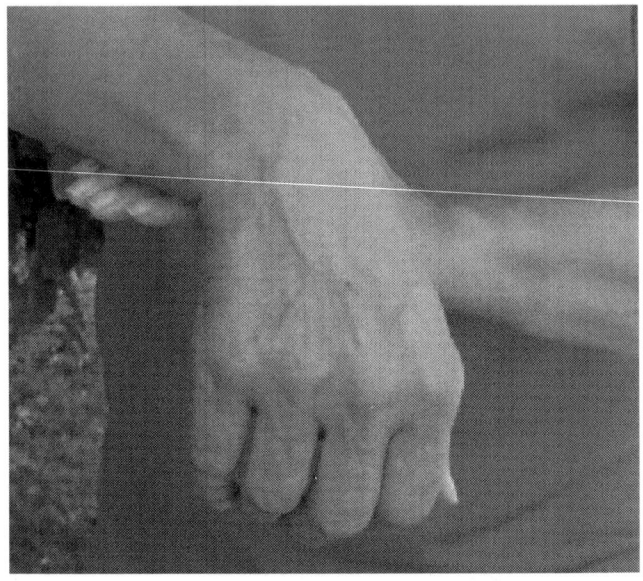

Next we continue what will become a fluid movement with a little practice. Slide the back of your right arm to the right until you overlay all the fingers of the left hand with your underside right arm. Your right hand palm and fingers still extend out beyond the fingers of the left hand. Stop when your right hand is in a position where, when you pull it back across, the thumb will once more glide directly over the top of the knuckles just beyond the wrist.

Make sure you have not straightened, nor sought to extend any fingers. Both hands must stay relaxed in the complete process for the best results. Keep your thumb up against your fingers much like the "ball" shape you made when you felt energy earlier.

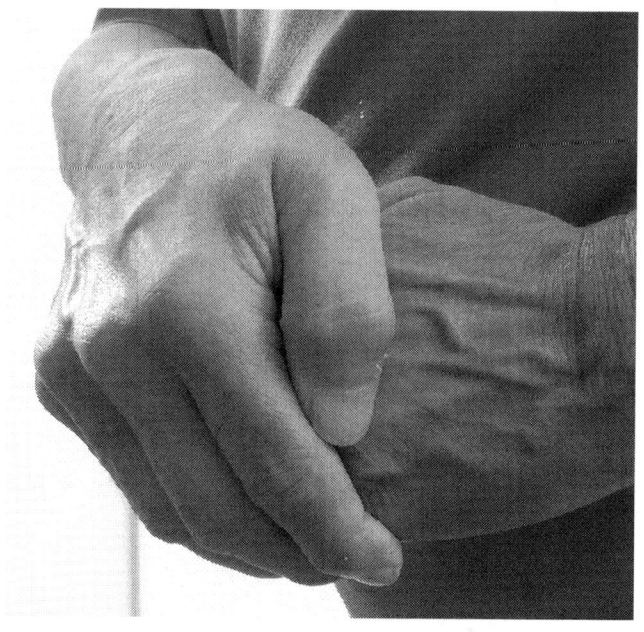

Begin to glide the contact surface of your right hand back across the knuckles and joints on all the fingers and ultimately the thumb of your left hand. Your hand will come all the way until the finger tips are once more at the edge of the left hand and slightly down from where they started. The best alignment coming back is to pay attention to your thumb while you bring your hand back and your thumb covers all the knuckles beyond the wrist like your little finger did earlier. While that is happening, the wrist and the knuckles of your right palm hand are now rubbing all the fingers and knuckles of your left hand.

Note: You do not move your left hand while learning the process. It should remain steady while your right hand does the clockwise pattern movement. Most people hold the hand being rubbed in the air and slightly in front as they look at their hands. That way you get to see the alignment of the little finger going over and covering the knuckles and the thumb doing the same coming back. The key is being "loose and relaxed" while the right hand does the clockwise rubbing rotation. You can think of it like applying a lotion all over the back of the hand. When you apply a lotion, you keep your hands relaxed. In this way you "feel" it all and that is most important.

Everything from here is a repeat of the steps above as you slide your fingers back to the starting position.

You have now completed the *Soul Link* movement process for one right hand palm pass over the top left. Now consider that you basically have designed the action to be like a box as you go across, slide down, and come back across.

When you learn this technique, it is important that you are able to do the steps almost without thinking about them. For this reason, you need to practice repeating the motion process of *Soul Link* until you know exactly what you are doing, and until it is one smooth movement. The necessary feelings of connection will work when you know the process and make it feel natural so that you can pretty much do it without thinking. Make it smooth and easy, remembering to "feel" all the connections you can.

Although you were told to read the whole chapter in the beginning, it is now time for you to stop and just learn this process until you feel it is a fluid movement for you, and that you know what you are doing when you slide over and glide back. When you ultimately use this technique, you will start and continue until you have made eight complete passes. It needs to begin with a full contact slide all the way past the palm, then a glide over, and all the way back. Sense all the feelings of connection as you create a continuous flowing motion.

Because of what you will soon read, it is best to stop and complete this part of the training before

continuing. You want success. I want to make healing memories as easy for you as possible. When you
can do this automatically, it will work best.

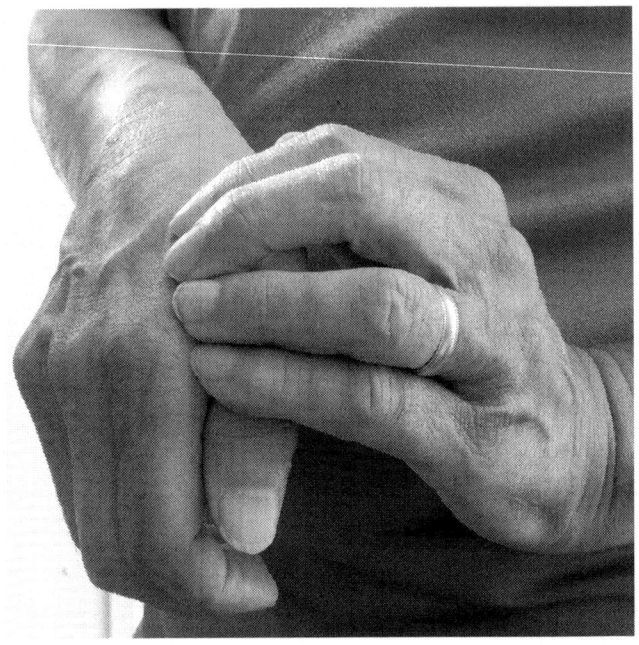

Now if I put a mirror between your hands and
you were ready to do the next step, you would merely
repeat it on the right hand doing the reverse of your
slide and glide pattern from the left. On the left
hand you went in a clockwise direction on the top of
the hand making eight complete patterns. On the
right hand top, you will go in a counter-clockwise
direction and do eight more complete patterns.

When you are comfortable that you can do it on
the right hand as smoothly and easily as you did on
the left, start checking how long it takes you to do

both sides. In the beginning the goal was just one continuous process so that I could make the slide and glide feeling work. It took about 30 seconds and was very much automatic. Once I started my hands moving, I just knew what to do, and I did not need to think about it any longer. If you are there, you are ready to learn the balance of the process of *Soul Link*. Today it takes me twenty seconds or less. It is not about the speed though; it is about the contact and the feeling of making contact happen automatical

~ Doing the Healing ~

From previous experience, you are aware of what memories are on a one to ten scale. For the initial run of this process, pick a memory with a negative charge in the three to five intensity range.

As you think about this memory, have some fun and play it in your head so that you can learn everything you can about it. Notice the sharpness, clarity, words, sounds, and feelings. What can you distinguish so that when you play it again later, you can check for differences? This will help with the quality of your first experience with *Soul Link*.

When you have learned all you can about this memory, place your right hand fingers against your left hand where you know the little finger is in line with the top knuckles. Now turn your focus as much as possible on all you recall as you repeat this memory while completing eight passes on each hand. Remember to do eight passes on both hands. A key component at this time is focusing your attention on the memory and not on how to move your hands. All hand movement should be close to automatic for best results.

When you are done, allow yourself to stop thinking about what you were doing and simply look around wherever you are and internally tell yourself some of the things you see around you. You need to stop thinking about the memory you were working on. Continuing to remember the memory is like sitting at an old fashioned switch board where all the cords are connected to your thinking from the time you start. By looking around now, you are basically pulling out the old cords and connecting in new ones.

It is time to check the memory. Think about it again and note if it is still at a three to five level. Try to note any changes that you can find to determine if this memory is still there and intact just as you remembered it before. Some will have a hard time finding the memory, and for some it may seem gone.

Check also to discover what has happened to the emotions and feelings that caused you to choose this memory in the first place. Is there anything there now? If there is, run the full pattern again as you pay attention to the emotions and feelings that now arise. I can tell you, however, with a three to five level memory, it is not normal for there to be residual that remains unless you paid more attention to the touch process than the memory content. Initially you may have a tendency to do that.

Give yourself another *Soul Link* test using another memory in the three to five range.

If you are satisfied with the change and are beginning to understand how good this *Soul Link* process is, choose a memory in the six to eight range and repeat exactly what you did before. Do the *Soul Link* process again. Make sure you run the memory until you are fully aware of what it is about and have garnered all the details possible including the picture, words, sounds, emotions, and feelings before running the process.

When you are fully aware of what you are doing automatically, do eight passes on each hand.

Remember to look around the room when you are done so that you can disconnect from what you chose to release. Then check the memory. What is different? Check the emotions and feelings next. Like before, are they now gone? In fact, for some of you the memory, as you recalled it, may also be significantly changed or gone.

Congratulations! You have learned to heal memories in seconds once more.

Short Check List
1. *Negative memory or just feeling*
2. *Soul Link process both hands*
3. *Look around to break connection*
4. *Check memory emotions and feelings*
5. *Memory should be neutral or do the emotions and feelings that have come up again*

What Can Be Done
with Soul Link

Experiment for yourself with a few more memories in the three to eight range, realizing that
most memories on a scale of one to ten are in the
eight and under range. I am not saying that you cannot go higher; the choice is yours. As you begin to
understand even more what this pattern is capable
of doing for and to you, listen to the desires of your
heart and your life will follow.

You might choose to just be present with a specific feeling or emotion and hold onto only that representation while doing *Soul Link*.

You might have pain somewhere in your body
and choose to focus on the discomfort while doing
Soul Link.

Test it in every way possible as it relates to you.
You are now at the controls of one of the greatest
tools ever created. You may discover that as you
think about a memory you desire to heal, it may only
take a few seconds to run *Soul Link*.

Once learned, many people go to only four passes on each hand and get the same results. I would not go below four passes. However, keep the amount of passes in good timing with how long it takes you to run the memory.

I could write a long list of all the things people have used this on and the varying degrees of memories they have healed. In some cases, what they healed changed their life completely. For some, what they discovered was like the tip of an iceberg where a new memory arose after doing the first recollection. In many ways, these memories were connected. In this case, they run the pattern again on what arises. They continue to do *Soul Link* until they realize they are only feeling peace.

For the first person I tested with PTSD, we did several memories and agreed to meet the following day. When I checked to confirm that we were still meeting, he wrote, "That thing you taught me yesterday works fantastic . . . going fishing!" The national disaster team leadership job he had been in force retired him because of his PTSD.

This author cried and thanked God for this gift to share with all.

It is a miracle to me. After thirty-four years of searching and creating therapy that works, I know well the tools you have just received. You now have the ability to actually heal memories in fifteen to thirty seconds! I have seen pain and many negative feelings gone in under ten seconds. There is nothing I have ever found that will do this. A drug can block a memory, however when it wears off, the memory is back with the attached emotions and feelings. *Soul Link* has the ability to help you change your life and create the life you desire.

I just returned from a teaching trip to Melbourne, Australia. In my time there, we counted over three thousand memories healed using *Soul Link* alone.

Why does it work? That is part of the teaching in *Restoration*. There I teach additional ways to break it down and use it for everything from "manifesting your desires" to "motivating yourself" to do something you just cannot get yourself to take on yet.

Today, four passes is all I use for myself. If something comes to mind, I do *Soul Link*. Or, someone says something to me that I realize is negative to them, and I just ask them to do what I do. Based on what appears to be the severity of what they are saying, four passes is what I use. Watching their face I can tell most heal even sooner. Learn for yourself what works best for you.

In working with people I meet casually, like the person next to me on a plane, I hear, "What did you do to me?" And things like, "This has been the most gut-wrenching thing in my entire life; now it does not bother me! What did you do?" Or things like, "I did weekly or monthly therapy for a decade. In two minutes with you, it no longer bothers me!" Then even more often I hear, "This is a miracle!"

Just yesterday I heard a girl say to her friend, "If you lived through what I did last month, you would understand why I think of suicide as the right thing so often!" In a few minutes I demonstrated *Soul Link*, then asked her to try it. With deep penetrating eyes she followed along repeating exactly what I was doing with my hands without disclosing any memory to me. Her last comment to me was, "Can I really use this on all the other stuff I have managed to live through? Can I really have a life again?"

I just completed a phone call with a doctor who said, "I am lowering my blood pressure with *Soul Link*! This is fantastic!"

Congratulations, you have learned to heal memories once more in seconds!

LAST WORDS

Having made it this far, and proved "***And can it be?***" to be possible for you. What is next?

There is a saying that goes, "You can lead a horse to water, but you can't make it drink!" I am praying you are now super thirsty to heal many memories as far back as you can remember.

My intent with this book is to open up your potential. Experiment with what you now know to be true. There is no such thing as failure. You cannot fail. Take that free moment in your day and heal a memory. Whatever comes up from now on, seek to discover which process works best for you. Hold onto any emotion or feeling that hinders your day and "use it energetically up" or use another process to neutralize it.

Inside, you are the energies of life. You are filled with energy of memories, relationships, generational pass-downs, and traumas along with other life sustaining and controlling energy. The processes you have just learned only scratch the surface with what I know is possible. I use this foundational knowledge to help people create change in themselves all the way to releasing, balancing, and neutralizing even that which is stored at an other than conscious level.

For twenty-plus years I taught *Life Clean Out* as a one-on-one program I created. I had researched every form of therapy that had to do with healing in mind, body, or spirit. Since 2008, I have taught *Life Clean Out* all over the globe in groups. The success of that change to groups has been equal to what it produced right from the start . . . Miraculous!

Significant changes have now been made to *Life Clean Out* so that it has been replaced by a newer two-day program called *Restoration*. It is still about all the change you can make to your life. The bigger memories, the other than conscious memories, karmic, genealogical factors, etc. are best addressed using *Restoration*. With this new format, it is possible for people to train to do *Restoration* with others.

It is no wonder that I get more "Thank You" cards around the holidays than I do specific holiday cards. *Life Clean Out* worked for thousands. Now *Restoration* works in one-third less time because of *Soul Link*.

So that you are aware of just some of what can take place in a *Restoration*, here is a potential possibilities list. Not necessarily will all take place each time, however most of it does. It really depends on where each person is in their life.

❖ Discover you have been Manifesting your whole life and know how and why
❖ Find yourself as Awareness in Consciousness and experience life as Spirit

❖ Discover the basic core reason and purpose you were born to live

❖ Fall in love with who you are on the inside as you learn to love yourself and become Love Living, not just Love Seeking, should you so decide

❖ Integrate all parts of who you are on the inside to the point where you recognize yourself as being in Wholeness

❖ Learn to live from your Highest Self in Wholeness as you move into Oneness/ Enlightenment

❖ Learn four major ways for healing negative memories all the way to potential success with PTSD

❖ Remove the foreign energy connections or control of others. Example: Learn how to live your life without proving your parents right or wrong any longer

❖ Find the root cause and/or the lessons associated with your major emotional reactions to life

❖ Release the energetic genealogical, karmic, and/or past life connections that no longer serve you

❖ Learn the laws of energy and attraction and how to design your future of service to others using the "desires of your heart" manifesting model

❖ Understand how to use thought to heal

❖ Learn how to make your blood flow in growth and regeneration rather than just protection so that you trigger "Remembered Wellness" to speed up healing and recovery

❖ Since thinking is the occupation of life, learn about the New Biology and Science of Epigenetics along with your part in the healing process using thought

❖ Most people look and feel ten years younger, as even your face reflects where you are at in life

For more information on Cyberphysiology and *Restoration* go to **www.GarySinclair.com.**

If you are a practicing therapist who would like to consider training to do *Restoration*, start your request through the web site.

Bless you — Heart to Heart with Infinite Love and Gratitude!
Celebrate Life!
Gary

ABOUT THE AUTHOR

Gary Sinclair first became interested in *Mind, Body, Spirit* work after recovering at age thirty-five in a year and a half from eighty percent mobility loss from fourteen years of Multiple Sclerosis. He had also slowly gone down to one-third lung capacity from birth defects and other complications. Six months after healing from MS, he miraculously received full lung capacity in fifteen minutes. He then went on to become a National Amateur Senior Olympic Gold Medal Figure Skating Champion for the USA and much more. There are even more miracles! Those who know Gary will tell you, "Gary is Love Living! He is what he teaches!"

For three decades Gary has researched the lessons related to all of life from his and others miracles. He has trained in all forms of energetic therapies. Out of his quest to discover how to help others, Gary created *CyberPhysiology* which is *Mind, Body, Spirit Training*. Just from a therapeutic stand point, Gary holds Master Certification in Neuro Linguistic Programming (NLP), Hypnotherapy, and Transpersonal Hypnotherapy, Time Line Therapy,™ Spirit Releasement Therapy, Soul Retrieval, Regression Therapy, Past-Life Therapy, Touch for Health, Bio-Feedback, Kinesiology, and much more in related energetic fields.

As a recognized leader in his field and his dedication to helping others, The National Association of Transpersonal Hypnotherapist and The American Board of Hypnotherapy awarded Gary the honor of "Outstanding Transpersonal Contribution in The Field of Bridging Mind, Body, Spirit" in 1996.

Gary has become accustomed to teaching and watching thousands of memories heal monthly as an international speaker. His training program, *Restoration*, is allowing people to have the tools necessary to become the person they always desired to be. *Soul Link*, in this book, is making many therapies obsolete.

Gary does not believe in miracles! He says, "People who say they believe in miracles, believe they are for others. I expect them and there is a difference!" He believes what many call supernatural is only the natural done in a super way. He is the author of two books currently in print, and several others that are out of print.

"Your Empowering Spirit: YES to Quantum Healing" (Seventeenyears in writing)

"Healing Alex" (Fictional story with healing training)

Gary currently resides in Southern California. He travels internationally as a gifted speaker and teacher. Many have been known to heal after listening to him teach.

Website: www.GarySinclair.com
Bookings arranged through the web site.
Restoration - Restoring Your Life, Re-designing Your Future.
Restoration two day training information on web.

Made in the USA
San Bernardino, CA
14 February 2016